Meditations
A Guided Journal for Women

Meditations

A Guided Journal for Women

Mindfulness Exercises to Inspire Your Practice

CAMERON KIELY FROUDE, PhD

ROCKRIDGE
PRESS

Interior and Cover Designer: Carlos Esparza
Art Producer: Janice Ackerman
Editor: Andrea Leptinsky
Production Editor: Jael Fogle
Production Manager: Jose Olivera

All illustrations used under license from Shutterstock

Paperback ISBN: 978-1-63878-483-8
R0

This journal belongs to

_____

Introduction

Welcome, my brave friend. By opening this book, you have entered a sacred space in our chaotic world. You are safe, loved, and accepted within these pages. You belong exactly where you are, right here on the opening page of a book that is designed to inspire you to transform your relationship with yourself.

My name is Dr. Cameron Froude, and I will be your guide as you learn about yourself through mindfulness and meditative practices. I am a medical family therapist with special training in trauma-informed approaches to healing. I've spent more than 10 years supporting high-functioning, perfectionist individuals as they learn how to heal from anxiety by integrating the wisdom of their mind, body, and spirit.

I developed the contents of this book in response to my own experience living with generalized anxiety, obsessive-compulsive disorder, and functional pelvic pain. After years of seeking answers outside myself, I decided to become my own healer. A core part of my healing included mindfulness and meditation. My body settled into a daily chanting practice, and my mind cleared during walking meditation. As each day passed, my values crystallized, and my spirit evolved. Finally, my life rested on a foundation of fortitude, focus, and fulfillment. I no longer sacrificed personal alignment for outward success. I then combined my new worldview with medical treatment that resonated with the needs of my body and spirit.

As women, we perform many roles. We cultivate our professional partnerships, romantic relationships, families, and communities. We are perpetual anchors for those around us. We are caretakers. We are hard workers. It is important we welcome restoration and rejuvenation into our lives.

This book will help you connect with your rich inner life. Your feminine wisdom will awaken as you practice quieting the megaphone of your thoughts and listening to the whispers of your body. The activities in this book are as diverse as the people who are reading this book. You will have the opportunity to engage your senses—sight, touch, smell, taste, and hearing—and experience the fullness of the world around and within you. You deserve these quiet moments.

Take a deep breath and find solace in being right here, in this moment, elapsing into the next and the next. In the next section you'll learn more about how to use this book according to your innate wisdom.

How to Use
This Journal

Developing a mindfulness practice is particularly daunting when you're in the throes of stress and anxiety. That's why I've developed a system for you to build a tailored mindfulness practice for your needs. This guided meditation journal offers concrete instructions on how to develop a mindfulness practice as well as dedicated spaces to reflect on what you have learned.

This book is organized into six sections that each explore a universal emotion:

sadness   fear
disgust   anger
happiness   surprise

You might want to amplify or soften these emotions—this book will assist you in doing both. Each section includes four methods for developing your practice:

Mindfulness-based practices are activities that you can do in your daily life when you aren't reading this book. These practices include somatic work, mindfulness activities, and restorative experiences.

Mindful meditations are five-minute meditative practices, including moving, sitting, chanting, and other approaches to meditation.

Prompts are brief questions or statements that invite you to examine aspects of your life from the everyday to the otherworldly.

Affirmations are concepts and beliefs that shift your mood and outlook on life. These are brief and powerful reminders of the strength that lies within you as a woman.

I believe in a truly integrated experience that centers mind, body, spirit, and relationships. Certain practices may be more or less difficult depending on your personal strengths and challenges. The moments when you struggle are opportunities to honor something about yourself. Be gentle with yourself as you explore the exercises in this book. Observe how you respond to certain prompts and activities. Your body and mind might speak loudly to you during some experiences. They might grow quiet during others. Listen with curiosity and humility to your holistic experience. My hope is that you will honor all parts of who you are through this process.

A
Gap

1. Bring to mind a disappointment you have experienced. This could be a friend letting you down. It could be a time you were upset with yourself. It could be a more expansive disappointment about the state of the world.

2. Take a piece of paper and fold it in half. On the left side, identify your expectations related to the disappointment. (For example, "I expected my friend to remember my birthday.") Fill that side with your expectations.

3. On the right side, identify the reality of what happened. (For example, "My friend sent me a card three days after my birthday. I felt pushed aside and forgotten.") Fill the column with what actually happened, including your own responses.

4. Open the page. The gap between the left and right columns is where disappointment grows.

5. Consider this question: How can I celebrate what actually happened while also honoring my unrealized expectations?

Parts of Disappointment

1. Invite the feeling of disappointment into your mind, body, and spirit. Feel its familiar ache. Recall its persuasive voice, showing itself as thoughts scrolling across your mind.

2. Attune yourself to the different parts of disappointment. You may feel a twinge of fear in your stomach. You might notice angry thoughts. Your spirit may feel tired. There might be several components of disappointment that exist for you.

3. Secure a piece of paper and colored pens or markers. When you conjure the different parts of disappointment, what color is each part? What shape and form do they take? Draw them.

4. Now draw lines that demonstrate how the parts relate to one another. For example, let's say you have a discouraged part and a worthless part. When a friend cancels plans, your discouraged part triggers feelings of worthlessness. To show that relationship, you might draw a lightning bolt between the discouraged and worthless parts.

5. Consider the relationships between these parts. Reflect on the relationships between parts you want to strengthen and those you'd like to weaken.

The Flame

1. Light a candle and sit or stand before it.

2. Breathe in deeply through your nose. Allow the air to travel down into your chest and farther into your navel. Breathe out. Repeat two times.

3. Name aloud something that is causing you a sense of sadness. Watch the candle and breathe deeply in and out, in and out.

4. As you watch the candle flicker, say the words "I release this sadness back to the universe." When you are ready, blow out the candle.

MEDITATION

I Can Be Anything

1. Stand with your legs apart, chin upright, and shoulders back.

2. Put your arms in a power pose, such as hands in the air, hands on hips, or arms out in an open embrace.

3. Whisper the words "I can be anything."

4. Repeat these words with increasing volume, remembering that you can choose to activate your strength and power.

5. Reduce your volume to a whisper, remembering that you can choose to preserve your strength and power.

Breathing Life into You

1. Sit or lie down in a comfortable position. Breathe in and exhale. Scan your body and identify the places where sadness is present. This is often in the abdominals, chest, and throat.

2. Give your sadness permission to emerge from your body in the form of tears, sounds, or words. If it does, thank it. If it doesn't, reassure it.

3. Breathe life into the sadness that exists in your body. Focus on bathing it in oxygen.

The Color of Sadness

1. Sit or lie down with a straight back, chin upright. Picture the sadness in your body as a color.

2. Take a deep breath through your nose, drawing the air from deep within and below your belly button.

3. When you exhale, push your stomach toward your back as if someone is pushing your belly button. Push the sad color into the air.

4. Continue pumping your belly button in and out for as long as your body feels comfortable.

Posture

Bring awareness to your posture. Consider the ways in which your body holds sadness. Where do you feel the weight? How would you describe the history of this sadness? Describe the first time your body and spirit held a profound sadness.

Channel

My body is a channel for light, and I choose the ways I present to myself and to the world.

Void

We often focus on what is immediately present, such as an emotion we feel, a task we need to complete, or a pain in our bodies. Consider what is not present. What emotion is not around? Who is absent? What task are you free from completing?

Space

I am as attuned to absence as I am to presence. I rejoice in the blank spaces of my life.

Suffering

We often suppress painful parts of the human condition.
Pay attention to the suffering within and around you. How do you tune in to others' pain? What do you hear and see? How does your perspective change when you consider suffering as a universal experience?

Embodiment

I show my strength by holding the suffering of the world, healing what I can, and relinquishing the rest.

Yearning

Yearning is an indication that you desire change. Pay attention to the times when you feel the stir of yearning, such as a desire to connect with a loved one or change careers. What desires have you consistently ignored throughout your life? How do you honor your current desires?

Recognizing Joy

I equally rejoice in the blessings I have and the yearning for gifts I have not yet received.

Fluidity

Be mindful of how you relate to the different parts of your identity. Do you strongly identify with a way of being, like assertiveness or confidence or sentimentality? How about with a particular worldview or political leaning? What happens when you consider adopting a new way of self-identifying? What becomes available when you leave space in your identity for change?

Transform

My personhood morphs, my body transforms, my spirit evolves. I embrace the only certainty: change.

Transitions

Packed days can leave us exhausted and overwhelmed. Plan a day where you leave time to care for yourself during transitions like commuting to and from work, preparing a meal, or drifting off to sleep. Reflect on what was gained in expanding time to care for yourself and transition. How did creating space for mindfulness impact your wellness?

AFFIRMATION

The Spaces Between

Transitions are the spaces where I gather myself and prepare for life's next blessing.

Hear

Disconnection from others fosters sadness. The next time you ask someone a question, listen deeply with the goal of understanding. Focus on the person's body language and posture. Resonate with their emotional state. How did it feel to listen with the goal of understanding? What did you learn that surprised you? How will you continue this practice?

Listen

I build meaningful relationships by listening for the values and aspirations hidden in plain language. I bring out the best in those who confide in me.

Reconnecting with My Body

Sadness can overcome us when we do not feel at home in our bodies. When you consider your relationship to your body across time, what themes emerge? What teaching did you receive as a child about how to respect your body? How do you want to connect with your body today?

Returning

I return to my body again and again. My body is my home, and I care for and respect its offerings.

Instinct

Sadness can increase or reduce appetite. As you move throughout your day, pay attention to the way your gut communicates with you. Notice when it churns and gurgles. Recognize when it's quiet. What needs does your gut communicate? How do you respond? What intuitive messages does your gut hold?

Nourishment

My body requires nourishment to carry out my daily vision. I am committed to my life purpose; therefore, I feed my body.

Patience

Sadness can cause irritability. Feelings of impatience live first in our body through movements like a tapping foot or quick sigh. Our thoughts then reflect that impatience. Be mindful of the ways irritation manifests in your body. Catch yourself and redirect them. What did you learn about yourself? How does irritation impact the relationship you have to yourself and others?

Release Irritation

I am patient with all living things in my life. When irritation rises, I breathe deeply and allow the exhalation to guide the impatience out of my body and mind.

Observing Disgust

1. Disgust is a feeling of repulsion or strong aversion elicited by something unpleasant. For example, a person may feel disgusted by a perceived foul odor, reprehensible behavior, or gross injustice. In some cases, disgust motivates health-related behaviors like sneezing into a tissue or washing hands after using the bathroom. Other times disgust can invite judgment, which can alienate us from others or ourselves.

2. The next time you feel disgusted, stop and observe this often-ignored emotion. What is the purpose of the disgust? Is this emotion serving a function that helps you stay healthy, alienates you from others, or something else?

3. Invite yourself to observe disgust from a distance. Remember that you can use disgust to facilitate new behaviors and/or reflect on your own judgment toward yourself or others.

Naming Disgust

1. Bring to mind a time you were disgusted by the way someone treated you.

2. Go outside and find a rock with a flat surface. On one side of the rock, write something or draw an image that reflects the experience. An example could be "When my partner lied to me." On the other side of the rock, write or draw a way of being that fills you with pride. An example could be "Patience."

3. Choose what you want to do with the rock. Some people keep it as a reminder of who they want to be. Others give the rock (and memory) back to nature.

Physical Release

1. Take a moment to tune in to your five senses—touch, taste, smell, sight, and hearing.

2. Identify an item for each sense that brings you comfort and calm. For touch, this might be a piece of Velcro or the corner of a soft blanket. For taste, this might be a butterscotch or peppermint lozenge. For smell, this might be a cotton ball saturated with perfume or lavender oil. For sight, this might be a beloved picture or magazine clipping. For hearing, this might be a seashell to put to your ear.

3. Bring these items together and place them in a small bag. Carry the bag with you and utilize these tools when you are stressed or overwhelmed.

Community

1. Pull up an Internet browser and start your own search for communities of people who share your experience and interests. Start with finding three, and be sure to bookmark them.

2. Engage with people from those communities. Engagement could include activities like attending an in-person support group, posting anonymously on a message board, or placing a phone call to someone you meet in your search.

3. Reflect on the ways that building community through a shared experience shifts the way you perceive yourself. How did you help someone else change their self-perception?

Small
to Big

1. Recall a time when someone made you feel small and insignificant.

2. Embody the way you felt at that time. This could mean slumping your body over a chair. It could mean bowing your head. You could sit on the ground with your body in a ball. Feel the constriction in your chest, the tightness of your limbs.

3. Very slowly expand your body, making yourself as big as possible. Notice the fullness of your breath and the change in your emotions.

MEDITATION

Value
Chant

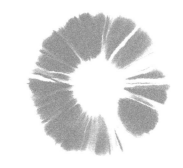

1. Choose a value-based word that you aspire to embody, such as "love," "wisdom," or "peace."

2. Find a comfortable place to sit or lie down using a blanket and pillow. Set a timer for 10 minutes.

3. Repeat the word again and again, allowing yourself to get lost in the rhythm.

4. When the timer sounds, rest for a few minutes and enjoy the quiet of your mind.

MEDITATION

Play

1. Sit or stand. Clap your hands or stomp your feet at a quick rate five times for three rounds.

2. Repeat. But this time, smile widely and say "ha" as you clap or stomp.

3. Now breathe deeply and laugh as you exhale. Perform three rounds of five breaths and five laughs.

4. Reflect on the remainder of your day. How can you integrate playfulness into it?

MEDITATION

Sight

1. Choose an item that holds significance for you. Sit in a comfortable place with it.

2. Set a timer for three minutes.

3. Breathe deeply. Close your eyes and feel the object. Notice the edges and surfaces. Bring the object to your nose and revel in its scent. Rub the object against your cheek or palm. Hold the object to your ear.

4. What thoughts or memories show up when you relate to this object with your senses?

Values

Reflect on the last several times you felt disgusted. What specifically was it about those situations that caused you to feel disgusted? When you consider your reason for feeling disgust, what do you identify as your core values?

Beliefs

My core values are the compass of my life. I shift my life path to honor my most deeply held beliefs.

PROMPT

A Loved One

Identify someone whom you have acted unkindly toward.
Close your eyes and picture that person. Open your chest and
place both hands on your heart. Write that person a letter
describing and honoring three of their best attributes.

AFFIRMATION

Self-Forgiveness

I forgive myself for prior unkind acts toward others. It's okay
to make mistakes, and I will know better from today forward.

50

Your Days

Consult your calendar and reflect on how you spent the past month. What activities, experiences, and people made you feel inspired and excited? How about depressed and unmotivated? Where did you feel safe and secure? With whom did you feel most protected?

Friendship

The world holds many opportunities. I seek experiences and people who create safe spaces for me.

Behavior

One motivation for engaging in a certain behavior is to pre-serve an important relationship. For example, a person might lie to their partner for fear of facing an angry response and potential breakup. Are you behaving in ways that don't reflect your values due to fear? If you changed your behaviors, who or what might you lose? What could you gain?

Clarity

I face my fears swiftly and directly. I speak with clarity to myself and those in my community.

Avoidance

Avoidance is a common response to uncomfortable emotions. Examples of avoidance include minimizing, dissociating, and denial. What emotions are you currently avoiding right now? How is avoidance serving you? How is it causing distress?

Confront

I am attuned to the ways I avoid and will commit to face my life when I am ready and with support.

Approaching Objectivity

Our self-assessment can be skewed by negative self-beliefs, such as "I'm not good enough," and by an inflated sense of self, such as when we tell ourselves, "I'm the best." Describe your strengths and areas of growth with as much objectivity as possible. What do you notice about yourself that was previously clouded by bias?

Lenses

I examine the lens through which I see the world. I am more than my biases, and therefore I seek to uncover them.

Navigating Pain

Suffering is inevitable, so instead of attempting to end suffering, we must navigate it. How do you relate to your own suffering? How about the suffering of your loved ones? How could you begin to navigate suffering in yourself and others?

Following

I am an anchor for my loved ones. I trust they know what is right for them, and I invite them to lead.

Ambivalence

Ambivalence occurs when someone has contradictory emotions about a person or experience. For example, a person might desperately want to stop drinking but continue to drink for fear of withdrawal. What areas of your life cause you ambivalence? How do you feel about holding contradictory emotions?

Contemplation

Uncertainty is an indication that I should stop and reflect on my next choice. I deserve a moment to contemplate.

PROMPT

Your Space

Our environment influences our mood. When you look around the spaces you occupy, like your bedroom, bathroom, or workspace, what do you notice? How can you change your physical space to reflect your preferred mood? What must change so you can maintain spaces that are clean, organized, and inviting?

AFFIRMATION

Tidy

I keep a clean house as a reflection of the order within my mind and the stillness in my spirit.

Last Meal

Our relationship to food can bring up a range of emotions.
Take a pause and bring to mind your last meal. What thoughts
immediately come up? What shows up in your body? What
would you like to change or maintain about the ways in which
you nourish yourself?

Mindful Eating

**Meals are a time when I enjoy the taste of food, rest my brain
from activity, and meet the needs of my body.**

Daydreaming

We can get lost in daydreams about alternative realities.
These could include changing jobs, starting a new relationship, or fleeing to a tropical island. When are you most inclined to get lost in daydreaming? What are you trying to escape in these moments? How could your daydreams become your reality?

Powerful Imagining

I daydream to enjoy the present moment and relish in the power of my imagination.

I Honor You

1. Bring to mind a person in your life whom you appreciate but have not directly thanked. Remember a time when that person did something kind for you.

2. As you recall that experience, engage with the emotions that arise. Where are they located in your body? Place your hand where you feel an emotion.

3. Breathe deeply and funnel the air to that emotional place in your body. Allow that emotion to grow and evolve, feeling it disperse across your entire body. Exhale.

4. Hold the person in your mind's eye, and envision in detail their good deed. Notice their mannerisms and the way you received their generosity. Watch yourself thank them in your imagination. Revel in their response to you.

5. Honor that person today. You could choose to share your mindfulness experience with them. You could bring them tea. You could include them in a prayer.

Meet Your Happiness

1. Envision a sacred being that exemplifies happiness in your life. Bring this being into existence. You could create this being using clay or Play-Doh. You could draw this being. You could simply imagine it. How does it look? What is its texture? What are its behaviors and habits?

2. Allow this being to come alive in whatever form makes sense to you. Give this being a name and a history. When was this happiness born in your life? Did it disappear for a while? How did it return?

3. Close your eyes and extend your hands. Hold your being of happiness gently in your palms. Feel its weight, shape, and texture. Allow it to move on your hands, up your arms, and onto your shoulders. Let it play on your head.

4. Store your happiness being somewhere you feel is safe.

Safety
Scent

1. Think of a scent you treasure. It could be a flower from the garden. It could be a spice that reminds you of your childhood home. It could be your grandmother's perfume. It could be your partner's well-worn sweatshirt. Take this item in your hands.

2. Sit or lie down in a comfortable place in your home. Breathe in the scent of the object. Notice the memories that emerge. Connect with the emotions of those memories. Notice the sensations of your body. Allow your body to relive the joyous moments connected to that scent.

3. Repeat the process several times until your body is completely relaxed. Say aloud, "This scent brings happiness into my being."

4. Pairing a calming scent with a stressful situation will decrease your distress. Consider a painful memory or a future fear. As you think about this distressing topic, breathe in your beloved scent. Say aloud, "My happiness is stronger than my pain."

MEDITATION

My
Love
for You

1. Sit in a comfortable position and picture a being that evokes peace, such as an animal or child. Look at that beautiful being and smile.

2. Breathe in through your nose and out through your mouth. Put your hands on your heart, and feel the beat for that beloved being.

3. Allow your body to experience the expansive love and connection you have for the being before you. Open your palms and expand your chest.

MEDITATION

The
Sound of
Happiness

1. Stand, sit, or lie down in a comfortable place. Recall a time when you were happy, or imagine an experience that invites happiness.

2. Allow your imagination to delve into that happy memory.

3. Open your mouth and allow your vocal chords to pair a sound with that memory. It could be a light hum, a song lyric, a loud sigh, or anything else that feels right.

4. Repeat that sound as you experience happiness in mind, body, and spirit.

The
Child
within Me

1. Go to the far end of a room or outdoors. Vigorously shake your arms and legs. Laugh and smile.

2. Pretend you are a carefree child. If you have never been that child, imagine a blissful child and embody her.

3. Move your body as that child would move. Skip, jump, play, somersault.

4. Lie on the floor or grass. Breathe in deeply and exhale. Enjoy feeling fun and free.

Energize

Play an upbeat song. As you listen, scan your body from head to toe. What do you notice? How does your body want to move to the music? Consider the thoughts running through your mind. Tune in to your emotions. How do you feel?

Smile

My lips are the channel to my deepest sorrow. They are also the door to my greatest joys. I choose to sing with pride.

Mind-State Change

Changing the state of your body changes your mood.
Close your eyes and smile widely. Recall a time when you laughed with someone you love. Open your eyes. Write a brief description of your change in mood. How does this exercise empower you?

Laugh

I laugh and my body relaxes, my emotions dance, and my thoughts halt. I create harmony through humor.

Thank You

Think of someone for whom you are deeply grateful. Choose someone you can meet in person or through a video call. Write a letter expressing your gratitude, indicating how the person's presence positively impacted your life. Arrange a visit and read the letter aloud to them.

Connect

I am one word—one embrace, one call, one breath—away from connection. I am someone who reaches out to love.

Authoring My Life

We write our life narrative. You are living the story you have written about yourself and for yourself. Use the present tense and write a narrative about the role of happiness in your life today. How do you envision your next chapter?

Authorship

My life is a tale I've written and edited a thousand times. And I will edit it a thousand times more.

A Present to Future Me

We live today to enjoy our present self, to heal our past self, and to prepare our future self. Describe something that your future self will need or desire. Consider the needs of your mind, body, spirit, and relationships. Create space in your day to do something for your future self.

Every Self

I am every past self I've outgrown, the present self I embody, and all future selves to come.

Connecting to Nature

We are part of nature. Open a window or go outdoors. Approach a part of nature that your body is drawn to, such as a tree or stream. Describe this part of nature in vivid detail—how does it taste? Feel? Does it make a noise or have a smell? Reflect on the ways you and this part of nature are inextricably connected.

Protection

My skin is the blanket that protects my body from harm.
I care for my skin as it cares for me.

Skin Care

The skin covering our body is our largest organ. Identify an area of skin that calls for attention, whether because of dryness, itchiness, or other distress. Mindfully clean and moisturize the area. Reflect on the ways your skin became distressed. Which other parts of your body would benefit from caretaking? Explain how you can improve care for your body each day.

Caretaker

I care for my body's casing by facilitating its regeneration through cleansing, moisturizing, and bathing. I am the keeper of my body.

Space

Empty space is freeing. Find a cluttered space in your home, like a drawer, cabinet, or closet. Empty all the contents onto the floor. Examine each item and decide whether to donate, regift, trash, or keep it. What becomes available to you with this new space?

Opportunity

I control the clutter and chaos of my life. I choose to create space in my home, heart, spirit, mind, day, and relationships.

Letting Go

We can take responsibility for actions that were never ours to repent. Think of something you hold emotions for that does not belong to you. How did you inherit this responsibility? How has it weighed you down? What will be free when you let it go? Write a letter that grants yourself permission to forgo that responsibility.

Give Back

I hold what is rightfully mine and return what belongs to another. From where it originated, it shall be returned.

Free Yourself

Remember an old song that brings you joy and happiness.
Play that song and allow your body to move freely. Sing loudly.
Laugh. If possible, dance with a pet or loved one. Reflect on
what becomes available emotionally when you free yourself.

Vessel

**My body is a vessel for unbridled joy, and I will transport the
passion of the world.**

We
Thrived

1. Gather the necessary items to write a letter to a very special person. You can design your own stationery, purchase a special sheet of fancy paper, or write in a beloved journal. Grab your favorite pen or special marker.

2. Think of a time in your life when you felt particularly frail and vulnerable. Close your eyes and reflect on that younger version of yourself. What were her deepest fears and desires? What did she desperately need to hear? How did she demonstrate her pain in the moment and her desire for something different?

3. Breathe in through your nose and out through your mouth. Grip your pen. Feel the weight of it. Acknowledge the gravity of this letter.

4. Write a letter to your younger self. Share with her the words that no one was willing or able to tell her. Connect with her in ways she needed but didn't receive.

Heal
Fear

1. Choose a part of your body that you know holds fear, which is a heightened state of stress. Fear can look like pain, aching, numbness, tightness, and other discomfort. These sensations often live in the abdomen, chest, lower back, neck, or head. Focus on a body part that needs peace. This part of your body has been strong for too long.

2. Sit or lie in a comfortable position, gently closing your eyes. Take several deep breaths, allowing the oxygen to breathe life into all parts of your body.

3. After several deep breaths, channel your breathing into the body part you have chosen to honor. Breathe vitality into that body part.

4. Allow your mind and spirit to connect with that body part. What emotion does it need right now—kindness, joy, reverence, faith, hope, love, or something else?

5. When you open your eyes, thank that body part for the strength it has provided you.

Release the Bottle

1. Consider something you have kept bottled inside due to fear of saying it aloud. This could be the name of a deceased loved one. It could be a trauma you endured in secrecy. Maybe it's the confession of a personal wrongdoing.

2. As you conjure the words, notice the reaction from your body and mind. Where does your body hold the emotion of the words? How is your mind influencing your emotional response? What is the core emotion you feel as you consider these words?

3. Breathe in deeply. As you exhale, say, "I calm my body through breath." Repeat this until you've brought your body and mind to a calm state.

4. Now speak aloud the thing you have kept bottled inside. When your body or mind become activated, bring them to a calm state again.

5. Repeat this process until your body and mind remain calm as you speak your truth.

Fear, Be Gone

1. Imagine fear and bring an image of it to your mind's eye. It could be a spiky orb or a gray cloud. It could be a symbol or an animal.

2. Close your eyes and ball your hands into fists. Bring your fists up with your knuckles facing you.

3. Open your fists and push the fear away as hard as you can. Tell the fear, "Be gone!"

4. Repeat and watch fear melt, disintegrate, and fly away.

Presence over Fear

1. Stand or sit at the far end of a room. Picture something you fear at the other end of the room. Remind yourself that you are safe.

2. Picture the thing moving toward you. When you feel fear in your body, direct the thing to stop approaching. Take a breath and relax your body. Direct the thing to continue moving toward you.

3. When you allow the thing you fear to reach you, greet it. Shake its hand. Fist-bump it. You are in control.

Invitation

to

Courage

1. Sit or stand with your arms out and palms facing the sky. Turn your face toward the sky. Open your chest.

2. Identify an image of courage. This could be an animal, a person, a symbol, or a color.

3. Imagine that image hovering just above your hands.

4. Repeat aloud, "You are welcome here," until you feel your body relax.

5. Draw your hands to your chest, and feel the beat of your heart.

Decisions

Consider five of the biggest decisions you have made throughout your lifetime. How did fear influence these life choices? If you had to do it all over again, what role would fear play in those decisions? How do you relate to fear today?

Peace

Peace comes easily to me. I channel my fear into focus. I transform my focus into action. I celebrate my successes.

Reacting to Fear

Remember a time you felt fear as a child, a teen, and an adult.
How did your body's reaction to fear change over time? How
about your thoughts? Behaviors?

I Am

I am me. I am braver than anxiety running through my body.
I am stronger than fear crossing my mind.

The Legacy of Fear

Fear can be passed across generations through things like storytelling, genetics, and shared experiences. Intergenerational fear could include historical trauma, like the effects of colonialism. It could also include incest, substance abuse, illness, and other experiences. What fears did you inherit?

Path

My ancestors built a path from their lives to my doorstep. I am ready to continue our journey.

Influence of the Other

Fear can stem from concern about how others perceive us. When you reflect on your fears, how much do they center on other people's opinions? What would be the worst perception someone could have of you? Does that perception change who you really are?

Become

I am not of others' design. I am who I become each morning. I am who I put to rest each evening.

The Origins of Fear

Chronic fear often results from a distressing event. Consider something you fear in your professional life or in a key relationship. What is the origin story of those fears? Why did that fear stick around?

My Birth

My origin story is infinite and pure. The child I once was still lives within me. My inner child and I are one.

Engaging from a Place of Fear

Identify something in your life that evokes fear. If you continue to relate to that thing from a place of fear, what will your life look like in one year? How about five years? Fifteen years? On your deathbed?

Departure

I will leave this earth, my community, and my loved ones richer than how I found them.

Fear as Acceleration

Under the right circumstances, fear can be a massive accelerator. It can feel a bit like nervous excitement, which can get us ready to make moves. Consider the different areas of your life, including school, work, parenting, and friendship. How has fear motivated you to act in one or more of these domains? What did you do to channel fear into action rather than freeze?

Shape-Shift

I transform my jittery stomach into a buzz of full-body excitement. Anticipation is the flip side of anxiety.

Bounce Back

Conquering fear requires the agility to bounce back after you stumble. This is called resilience. How quickly do you bounce back from setbacks? What is your process for recovering from failure and getting back on your feet? How could you practice resilience this week?

Float

I am a buoy. No matter the size of the wave or the pull of the current, I will emerge.

The Body's Alarm System

Fear can be a natural warning sign for danger. It can also be a false alarm. Is there someone in your life who incites fear in you? When you reflect upon that relationship, what message are you addressing, ignoring, and/or amplifying with your fear?

Control

I control my life, my body, and my spirit. You will never take me over again. I will not allow it.

Fear as a Tool

We can use fear as a mechanism to control people and situations. Do you use fear to assert power and control? If so, who taught you that way of being? Does it feel in line with who you want to be?

Peacemaker

I convert fear responses into compassionate contributions and gentle requests. I am a peaceful communicator who seeks collaboration with others.

Redirect Anger

1. You will need a bar of soap and either a sink or a bowl with water.

2. Bring something to mind that evokes anger. Channel that anger into the soap by picturing a red stream going from your body into the soap. You can imagine the anger funneling through your fingers and eyes.

3. Wet your hands. Take the soap and massage it into your hands. Watch the soap foam on your hands. Create friction to increase the bubbles. Stay present to the anger that was funneled from your body into this soap, which is now on your hands.

4. Rinse your hands and watch the suds swirl down the drain. You have rid yourself of anger by inviting it to emerge from your body, channeling it into another object, funneling it to your hands, and now washing it away.

Space
to
Choose

1. Think about a time when you felt mildly angry. Allow those feelings to emerge in your mind and body. Let's practice creating space between that emotion and your response.

2. Make a cup of tea with concerted mindfulness. Focus on each and every step. Turn on the kettle. Choose your favorite mug. Smell the tea bag and drop it into the mug. Wait for the whistle. Pour the water.

3. As you sit and wait for your tea to steep, feel the heat on the side of the cup. Smell the tea and feel the slight moisture on your nose from the heat. Be present to your experience.

4. Return awareness to the angry experience. Consider how you want to respond.

Self-Compassion

1. Identify a time when you were angry at yourself. Self-anger can elicit strong feelings of shame. Regardless of whatever you think you did wrong, you deserve compassion. Releasing anger toward yourself requires forgiveness.

2. Picture a young child who you love, either real or fictional. Imagine this child standing in front of you. As you imagine this child in great detail, be present to your emotions and physiology. For example, you might feel adoration and warmth in your chest.

3. If that child performed the same behavior you did or a similar one, how would you respond? If the child indicated they felt ashamed and angry at themself, what would you say or do to comfort them? Speak those words aloud to the imaginary child in front of you.

4. Look in a mirror. Speak the same words you said to that child to yourself.

Summon Anger and Release It

1. Anger is an emotion that comes and goes. Give yourself permission to feel anger.

2. Breathe in deeply. Hold it. Exhale. Repeat three times.

3. Breathe in and scrunch your shoulders up to your ears. Pause for three seconds.

4. Exhale and let out a growling sound. Notice your emotions. Feel them float across your body. Notice your thoughts. Allow them to pass through your mind.

5. Repeat steps 3 and 4 until the anger is released.

Release

1. Identify a place in your body where anger resides. Anger often lives in the neck, shoulders, chest, and fists.

2. Breathe in deeply and tighten that part of your body. Hold your breath and then exhale, releasing that body part.

3. As you breathe in again, whisper the name of the body part. When you release, envision the anger shooting through your arms and out the tips of your fingers.

4. Repeat until calm.

MEDITATION

Angry Vibrations

1. Close your eyes and consider something or someone who kindles anger within you. Notice where the anger is located in your body.

2. Allow the anger to emerge from your throat and mouth. Make a sound that reflects the anger; this could be a low hum, a shriek, a growl, or a cry. Give yourself permission to express anger.

3. Continue until the sounds become quieter and more rhythmic. Invite variations in your verbal expressions of anger.

Observing

Anger can be an emotion that notifies us of a violation of our boundaries. Reflect on the last time you felt angry. Was there a threat to your boundaries? How did anger assist you in reestablishing those boundaries?

Seeker

I am a seeker of light amid darkness. I see the good in all things I encounter.

Yes

Anger invites "no" into our lives. It shuts us down. Say "yes" aloud 10 times. Notice how your body changes. Recognize the power of yes in destabilizing anger's energy. How would your work, family, and social life change if your tendency was "yes"? What stops you from saying "yes"?

Manifestation

The power of yes is within me. I say "yes" because the world is available to me. I manifest abundance.

Path

Self-loathing emerges when we doubt our life path and decisions. The path you're walking today leads you to the perfect destination. How would you describe your path? Who walks beside you on it? Where has your path taken you thus far?

My Walk

My path is perfect for where I've been, where I am, and where I'm going. My life is a divine walk.

Justice

Anger can signal an injustice toward ourselves or others.
When you reflect on your life, when was the first time
you experienced injustice? How did your loved ones
and caregivers respond to injustice? As an adult, what is
your process for confronting injustice?

Advocacy

I am a conduit for fairness. I provide support to those who are
vulnerable and accept help when I need it.

Inner Child

Your inner child contains both happy and painful moments from your childhood. Close your eyes and picture a young version of yourself. What memories is your inner child holding on to? Is there a message your inner child needs to hear? How can you provide relief to your inner child?

Re-Parenting

I am a caretaker to my inner child. I assure that child that they are safe, loved, and protected. I am the parent I always deserved.

Seeing Myself

Shame and anger work together to alienate us from our core self. Take a mirror and make prolonged eye contact with yourself. What emotions emerge as you gaze into your own eyes? How do you think your loved ones see you? What difficulties emerge as you look into your eyes?

Soul

My eyes are the window to all that I've endured and the person who I've become. I fall in love with myself every morning.

Abandonment

Feelings of abandonment can evoke resentment and anger.
Pick a time when someone you loved left you feeling alone and forgotten. Write the details of the incident. What did you make that perceived abandonment mean about yourself at the time? How has that meaning changed since that time?

Belonging

I will always return to myself. My relationship to others is flexible, and I accept when people enter and exit my life.

Overflow

Bottled feelings lead to an emotional overflow. Often, we bottle emotions to avoid conflict. Choose a relationship to explore. How does your conflict style differ from the other person's? How do you share difficult emotions with each other? Where do you see opportunities for more authentic communication in this relationship?

Honesty

I express my feelings in the moment they emerge with a calm and intentional spirit. I will express my truths.

Jealousy

We can reduce the charge of jealousy by identifying our desires.
As you think about the people in your life, who evokes jealousy
within you? What exactly is it about their lives or personhoods
that you admire? How could you embody one of their admirable
characteristics in your own life and relationships?

Striving

**I admire others with full acknowledgment that I am never
lacking and also have room to grow.**

Bliss

Laughter eclipses anger. Use the internet to find a video of a person laughing. You can also imagine a laughing person. As you watch, focus on your experience. How does your face respond to the laughing person? What can you learn about the way your experience mirrors those around you?

Laughter

My laugh is contagious, and my personhood is rich. I connect with the hope that exists within each person.

A
Gift

1. Reflect on something you could do today that would really surprise your future self. Consider how your future self would benefit from this gift. What would it offer to you?

2. Take time to prepare this gift for your future self. It could be knitting a scarf for the winter. It could be going for a run in preparation for a 5K. It could be setting aside money for holiday gift-giving.

3. After you have completed the gift, thank yourself today for doing something kind for the future you.

Daily Wonder

1. Choose a routine activity in your day, such as preparing coffee, dropping your children off at school, or tidying the bedroom. Commit to finding the surprise in this activity the next time you engage in it.

2. As you engage in your routine activity, look for the wonder and amazement. When you quickly prepare a pot of instant coffee, consider the time it would take without electricity. As you tidy your bedroom, reflect on how deeply your younger self yearned for a room of her own.

3. If someone without your resources witnessed this task, how would they react? If your younger self saw you completing this activity, what would that young version of yourself think or say?

Surprise Another

1. Think of a relationship you're in, of any type, that you consider to be stuck in a rut. The ways we relate to people, particularly in long-term relationships, can become predictable. This is someone you feel more routine with.

2. Recall when this relationship became predictable. Can you remember when, or why?

3. When you reflect on the needs of this relationship, what could you offer to surprise your person in a deep and meaningful way? You could decide to call a friend you normally text. You might celebrate a coworker with whom you speak often. Maybe you invite your partner on a walk instead of lounging in front of the TV.

Good Morning

1. When you first open your eyes, stretch your arms and legs and take a deep breath. Treasure this moment in time. Look at the ceiling with your eyes open, allowing your mind to wander. Our day can be filled with gifts and surprises when we prime ourselves to see them.

2. Identify five experiences you want to have today. Say them aloud.

Joyful Place

1. Lie down or sit in a comfortable position. Bring to mind a place that fills you with joy, either real or imagined. Think of a meaningful experience you had in this place or imagine having.

2. Envision the details of that place. Welcome the emotions, sensations, and thoughts that connect you to this experience.

3. As you are imagining, tap your right knee and then your left knee very slowly, repeating about 20 times. Doing this will connect your mind and body as you conjure this special place.

MEDITATION

Mountain Pose

1. Stand or sit with your feet about six inches apart.

2. Tighten your core and pull your hips under just slightly. Shrug your shoulders and roll your neck to help the muscles let go and relax.

3. Inhale deeply and reach your arms above your head while keeping your feet firmly planted on the floor. You can also keep your hands at your sides and raise your chin.

4. Look above you, recognizing your inherent elation and bliss. Take long, deep breaths.

   Note: Visit VerywellFit.com for visual directions on how to do the mountain pose.

Excitement

When we feel excited, nervous, fearful, surprised, or anxious, our body responds. Our stomach fills with butterflies, and our heart rate quickens. When was the first time you experienced these sensations? How did that first experience shape the way you relate to your emotions today?

Evolution

I am constantly evolving and open to new experiences and ways of being.

Anchor

Anchors serve to ground our minds, bodies, and spirits during challenging times. When you reflect on your life, who have been your primary anchors? As you look around your physical world, where do you feel safe and secure?

Centered

I ground myself in self-confidence, community bonding, and connection to my environment. I determine my state.

Many Versions of You

Gather some colored markers or pencils. Draw an image, either real or symbolic, of yourself when you are overwhelmed by stress. Draw another image of yourself when you are calm and grounded. Draw a final image of yourself when you are depleted and drained. What do you notice about the differences in color, shape, and texture between the drawings?

Multiplicities

I exist in multiplicities. My power lies in my ability to transform stress and worry into calm and peace. My identity is composed of many elements.

Fun

Adults often lack opportunities to be fun and playful.
Consider the last time you really laughed, felt joyful, and
played. Who brings out the carefree side of you? How can you
connect with this person and broaden this social circle?

Child at Heart

I am in tune with my inner child and keep her close. I use my
strength and compassion to honor her at all times.

Quiet

External stimuli influence our thoughts and physical state.
Turn off all lights and sounds. Lie quietly and notice what
emerges. Now turn on all the lights and play an upbeat song.
Pay attention to what changed. What degree of sound and
lighting feels most comfortable? How can you tailor your envi-
ronments to match your sensory needs?

Habitat

**I deserve to lie in stillness, allowing the light and sound of
my surroundings to bathe my body in tranquility.**

Spontaneity

Surprises can trigger a variety of responses, such as unbridled excitement or overwhelming nervousness. What is your relationship to surprises? What are your early childhood memories related to surprises? How did these memories shape your responses today?

Anticipation

Each day I anticipate that surprises will unfold. I welcome spontaneity and embrace the unknown.

I Am Worthy

Say the words "I am worthy" out loud at least five times using different vocal tones. Which way of speaking these words was new for you? Which one felt most comfortable and fitting? Who in your life needs to hear these words, and how do you plan on sharing them with that person?

Voice

The energy in my voice fuels my message. I will speak my truth today and create space for others to do the same.

Rocking

Body rocking can evoke a calming state. Stand, sit, or lie down while rocking your body left to right and back about 20 times. How did this movement feel for your mind and body? When you think of a mildly stressful event and rock, how does your perception of the event change?

Presence

I give myself the care and attention I need to move through the day with full presence and engagement.

Mornings

You deserve to eagerly open your eyes each morning, anticipating the day ahead with unbridled joy. What is something that needs to shift for you to look forward to every day? How does your evening routine enhance or constrain your happiness in the morning?

Resolution

I am open to the messages the universe sends to me and will integrate them into my day.

Yet

Consider a way of being that has eluded you. For example, maybe you live with anxiety and seek calmness. I encourage you to say, "I am not calm *yet* . . ." Consider what you aren't *yet*. What becomes available when you add the word "yet"? How can you relish in the process of *becoming* rather than fixating on arriving?

Worth

I strive to be the best version of myself today and acknowledge my inherent worth in all that I do.

Conclusion

Congratulations! You have reached an important milestone and come to the end of this book. You invested in yourself and engaged in a host of activities and exercises to care for your mind, body, and spirit.

Completions can bring out strong emotions. Let's take a minute to check in about this journey:

- How has your body changed?

- What thoughts are present for you now?

- How would you describe your spiritual space?

Consider the end of this book as the beginning of your renewed mindfulness practice. This is the beginning of a lifelong relationship between you and yourself.

Planning for continued practice requires reflection on your current routines. When we create systems to mitigate our weaknesses and enhance our strengths, success is a given. For example, let's say someone struggles to make time for mindfulness practice. However, once seated, they have incredible focus. It might be easier for this person to engage in a mindfulness practice while carrying out a separate daily activity, like preparing breakfast or driving to work. Scheduling the practice alongside a routine activity reduces their risk of forgoing it and capitalizes on their ability to focus on the task at hand.

Consider the weaknesses and strengths of your mindfulness practice. Complete an honest self-assessment with pride in where you are and anticipation for where you're headed by asking yourself:

- What are the gaps in my practice?

- What are the most solid parts of my practice?

- What systems do I need to implement to close the gaps and shore up the strengths?

After you have engaged in this self-assessment, share your findings with your loved ones and community. Ask other people in your orbit to help support you in cultivating your mindfulness practice—they might even want to join your practice and learn from your journey.

You are a wise survivor with the whole wide world before you. I believe in your ability to connect deeply with yourself, your loved ones, and your environment. Take solace in the safe space you have developed in mindfulness. It's yours, and no one can ever take it away from you.

Resources

The Beginner's Guide to Stoicism: Tools for Emotional Resilience & Positivity by Matthew Van Natta

> *The Beginner's Guide to Stoicism* describes how stoicism can facilitate calmness. In this accessible primer, readers learn about the history of stoicism, the stoic mindset, and strategies to integrate stoicism into daily life.

Michelle's Sanctuary

> Michelle's Sanctuary offers guided meditations and sleep stories to help new meditators get in the groove and insomniacs drift off to sleep. The creator, Michelle, uses ASMR and other relaxation techniques to enrich her meditations. Visit YouTube.com/c /MichellesSanctuary.

The Mindful Way through Depression: Freeing Yourself from Chronic Unhappiness by Mark Williams, John Teasdale, Zindel Segal, and Jon Kabat-Zinn

> *The Mindful Way through Depression* combines perspectives from several experts and healing traditions to explain how mindfulness can reduce depression. An accompanying audio guide includes meditations the reader can use to enrich their practice.

The Miracle of Mindfulness: An Introduction to the Practice of Meditation by Thich Nhat Hanh

> Zen master Thich Nhat Hanh describes important tenets of mindfulness through storytelling and activities readers can try at home. He focuses on mindfulness in our everyday lives,

highlighting that even the most mundane tasks offer moments for self-enlightenment.

Omega Institute for Holistic Studies

The Omega Institute is a nonprofit educational organization that helps people and organizations practice social change. The Omega Institute's YouTube page is a rich resource, full of interviews with experts, yoga practices, and talks on a variety of wellness topics. Visit YouTube.com/user/TheOmegaInstitute.

The Power of Now: A Guide to Spiritual Enlightenment by Eckhart Tolle

The Power of Now is a guided self-help book that assists readers in finding inner peace through presence. By focusing mindfully on the here and now, readers learn how to access their mission and purpose.

The Power of Vulnerability by Brené Brown

Brené Brown, author, researcher, and professor, explains the role of vulnerability in self-development in this 2010 TEDxHouston talk. By intertwining people's stories with social science research, Brown artfully demonstrates how we can leverage vulnerability to uncover important lessons about our humanity.

Unify.org

Unify organizes community-based, synchronized mindfulness events. Organizers invite people from all backgrounds to engage in mindfulness practices like meditation, prayer, local ceremonies, and more.

Resources

Acknowledgments

For my mum and brother, who offer me a safe place to land at every turn. For my husband, who creates endless opportunities to celebrate this moment and dream the next into existence. For our kittens, Fenjoon and Duchess, whose soft purrs remind us to honor the power of the gentle breath.

About the Author

 Dr. Cameron Froude is the founder of Bliss In Being, a health care company that provides psychotherapy and coaching to individuals, couples, and families recovering from chronic stress and trauma. Dr. Froude earned a PhD from the Human Development and Family Sciences program at the University of Connecticut and completed a postdoctoral fellowship in Family Medicine Education at the University of Colorado School of Medicine. Dr. Froude is an EMDR-certified, licensed therapist and clinical supervisor. She has over 10 years of experience helping trauma survivors tap into their resilience and thrive in all areas of their lives. If you are interested in working with Dr. Froude, you can learn more at DrCammy.com.

CPSIA information can be obtained
at www.ICGtesting.com
Printed in the USA
BVHW020432130122
626109BV00015B/225